Workbook To Analyze People

Practical Exercises: Analyze Verbal Communication and Body Language — Persuade People — Control Mind

Dale McLeo

Table of Contents

Introduction

Imagine you're having a crucial discussion with someone—this could be a job interview or a date. The point is, you want to be able to decipher their verbal and nonverbal reaction to you.

No book can honestly promise that you'll be able to accurately figure out anybody's exact thoughts. But you can determine what emotions are at play and with that predict their next course of action. This is the closest you'll get to actually reading someone's mind, and this book discusses the various methods to go about it in a comprehensive and light-hearted manner.

But, being able to analyze people doesn't stop at reading verbal and nonverbal cues. You'll also learn how to persuade anyone you come across, control their minds, and protect yourself from manipulation.

This being a workbook, let's get straight to the point. Enjoy.

Chapter 1: Practical Exercises To Improve The Ability To Analyze Verbal Communication

Since communication is simply known as the act of using signals, signs, words or behavior to express ideas, thoughts, feelings and so on, it has turned out to be as crucial as the air we breathe. It is not difficult to understand why. Human beings will not exactly be who they are if they did not have the ability to communicate. Man thrives on the very fact that he can express his feelings and opinions whenever he needs or wants to. We see how crucial it is for man to communicate in how desperate a deaf or dumb, or deaf and dumb man is to get healed.

The inability to conveniently speak is regarded as a disability and a limitation. Although people who find themselves in such situations adapt quickly and learn other ways to communicate, the disability still quite limits them, one way or another. Animals make sounds to communicate with one another. And if they are domestic, to communicate with their owners.

A dog will bark to alert its owner of a stranger's arrival or something else that it feels its owner should see immediately. When they whimper, they are probably in pain, hungry, or just looking for attention. The same goes for other animals including man. Every species has its own unique way of communicating and passing important signals across. It is interesting, to say the least, that every animal in existence communicates in one way or another.

Man regards himself as a social animal. There's a desperate need for him to relate with others, to work with them. There's a need for understanding, love, care, companionship, and protection. These needs of his can only be met through communication.

The historical Tower of Babel was going to be the first "skyscraper" in history. The builders had one language and one interest. They could effectively communicate with each other and discuss a strategy. This made them simply unstoppable as they began the project and were not going to fail. The only way to stop them was to put in a communication barrier. That worked. Today, we have resorted to the use of official languages to bridge the gap of different native languages, so that we can still come together in worldwide activities like the Olympics, World Cup, writing contests, singing, dancing, art competitions, and others. Without the use of a common language, all of these would have been impossible.

For centuries, we have heard good things falling apart because of the inadequacy in communication between or among those involved.

A marriage, for example, thrives on the readiness and ability of the couple to communicate effectively. Both parties are expected to be able to honestly express their feelings to each other and say when they are hurt so things can be fixed. Leaving matters unattended to for a long time because the offended party does not communicate his or her displeasure eventually leads to the creation of a rift that inevitably continues to widen until they communicate.

In the workplace, an executive must understand the skills of effective communication in order to achieve his goals using human resources. The ability to correctly interpret the message in a piece of information is something largely relative to humans. This has to do with intelligence a lot of times, explaining succinctly the reason why in a classroom of twenty pupils, ten students will score highly on a test while the other ten will range between average and low marks on a topic that was taught them all by the same teacher in the same way.

Some parents are puzzled when a pupil considered weak in mathematics changes his teacher and begins to understand what he is being taught in the subject. Many conclude that the former teacher did not do his job well. While that is sometimes true, it is not always the case. We should ask questions like: What if the pupil did not like the teacher? What if the pupil was not used to the teacher's style? Man, being a complex animal, is not always compatible with every member of his species, and this sometimes impacts his likeability of the other person and in the long run, his accurate comprehension of whatever they ever try to communicate to him.

Thus, the preferred communication style is always an important factor to consider when deciding on compatibility with another person. The types of communication that exist, verbal, nonverbal, and written communications, are individually and altogether crucial to the thriving of man as a social being.

Man's temperaments have been divided into sanguine, choleric, melancholic and phlegmatic. Each of these temperaments has been found to have varying preferences for particular communication types. The sanguines who are regarded as extroverts prefer to use verbal communication and they do it ever so loudly. It has been said that a sanguine enters a room with his mouth first. He is usually loud and jovial, and often times very good at his use of words, successfully making people laugh and enjoy his company by and large. His humor has been found to be contagious, having the ability to see the funny side of every situation and discuss it in the funniest way. He loves public speaking and his loud voice is many times nice to listen to.

The choleric, who is a close relative of the sanguine, communicates well verbally. He is usually not as loud as the sanguine but can also use words well.

The introvert is the melancholy, he is most inclined to nonverbal and written modes of communication. Because he likes to keep to himself a lot of times, he does not speak as much as the sanguine and choleric do. He usually just finds his passion and immerses himself in it. Many times, that passion is in medicine, research, writing, arts or music. When he does use verbal communication, he uses it well.

The extreme introvert, the phlegmatic, keeps to himself more often than the melancholy does and his preferred mode of communication is similar to the melancholy. He is generally regarded as gentle and easy-going and so children warm up to him more easily. Depending on what category of temperament a person belongs to, they usually have a preferred way of communicating with fellow humans.

Verbal communication is greatly useful, convenient, and permits a lot of expressiveness. Emotions are more easily read when communication is done face to face. Nonverbal communication, on the other hand, involves the use of signs, symbols, facial expressions, eye signals, and body language to communicate. While it is not exactly sufficient to be used as a primary or singular mode of communication, it is adopted by some people because they are limited in their ability to use the other forms of communication due to a disability.

The inability to hear or speak limits them and in order to have the best of normal lives, they must learn how to communicate their feelings without speaking. That is, they must learn to use communication forms other than verbal. Animals such as gorillas are able to tell a man that they're scared by putting their palm over their chests and pretending to breathe heavily. Cats are said to be professing love to their owners when they gently open and close their eyes.

Nonverbal communication often enhances the efficacy of verbal communication. It is not just enough to be able to talk. People usually hear more than just the words that we speak. Our body language is very important to people and while we may be saying yes, our body language may say no and that makes us come off as actually unwilling or dishonest. For understandable reasons, people are more concerned about our overall body language than what we said in reality. They use our body language to judge if what we say is true.

Above nonverbal and written communication modes, verbal communication is chief. It helps convey messages faster, easier, and more clearly. Not that it is not possible to mince words and confuse the listeners, but it is easier to clarify things and faster, too. Verbal communication is adopted in health care, schools, churches, the workplace, and so on.

Verbal communication is a sum total of the sounds, words, language, and speech we use in communicating. Speaking is an effective method of communication and helps in expressing emotions in words. Verbal communication is divided into intrapersonal, interpersonal, small group communication, and large group communication.

Intrapersonal Communication

This is communication with oneself using internal vocalization or reflective thinking, because the ability to talk to oneself and think in words is a major part of the human experience of consciousness. It takes place in the mind of an individual. In such a situation, the person converses with themselves, either vocally or in their own heads. Usually, this is called 'self-talk' or 'inner speech'. This could take the form of a monologue or, even more peculiar, and internal dialogue.

No one is exempt when it comes to having internal dialogues. In such scenarios, place yourself in the position of both the first and second (or more) speakers and hold back and forth conversations—engaging dialogues no less. Funny though it might seem, it is commonplace.

Just like other forms of communication, intrapersonal communication is triggered by some internal or external stimuli. One may, for example, communicate with themselves about what they want to eat due to the internal stimulus of hunger. We may also react intrapersonally to an event we witness.

There are three aspects that govern Intrapersonal communication. They are:

1) **Self-Concept**: This has to do with what an individual conceives of themselves. There are three crucial factors at play here: beliefs, values, and attitudes.

2) **Perception**: This is what the mind makes of the external information received.

3) **Expectation**: This is what an individual believes or imagines would happen.

Intrapersonal communication serves several social functions. Internal vocalization, or talking to ourselves, can help us achieve or maintain social adjustment. Intrapersonal communication also helps build and maintain our self-concept. We form an understanding of who we are based on how other people communicate with us and how we process that communication intrapersonally.

We also use intrapersonal communication or "self-talk" to let off steam, process emotions, think through something, or rehearse what we plan to say or do in the future. Intrapersonal communication is the base of other types of verbal communication. Why is that, you ask?

This is because what goes on in our heads and the way we view ourselves (Self-Concept) largely informs our perception of the world. And whatever interaction we have with others will rely heavily on this.

Interpersonal Communication

Interpersonal communication is the process of exchange of information, ideas, feelings, and meaning between two or more people through verbal and/or non-verbal methods. It often includes the face-to-face exchange of messages, which may take the form of a certain tone of voice, facial expressions, body language, and gestures. The level of one's interpersonal communication skills is measured through the effectiveness of meaning transferred through the message.

In Interpersonal Communication, the tone of voice, body language, facial expressions, and others have a good chance along the way of determining how the other person will receive what is being said. They are as important as the words spoken.

Four factors are at play with interpersonal communication:

1. **Inescapable**: Whether you choose to speak or not, you will communicate something to the other person. Choosing to keep silent will say something about your mood, character, or nature.
2. **Irreversible**: If you've said it, then you've said it. There's no way to take it back
3. **Complex**: interpersonal communication is not often an easy or straightforward process. It requires explanations and careful listening to not misunderstand what is said.
4. **Contextual**: This is in relation to the point above. Whatever is said must be understood in its context, which could be environmental, political, psychological, etc..

Small-Group Communication

This involves interactions among three or more people who are connected through a common purpose, mutual influence, and a shared identity.

This small group is generally formed to solve a particular problem, make decisions, determine policies and submit reports. Personnel Committee, audit committee, report committee, and grievance committee are the example of small groups. Also, group assignments in schools usually feature small groups of students focused on solving their assignment questions or carrying out their joint projects.

A key advantage of small group communication is that information is easily shared as the communication is usually informal and unstructured. Small group communication usually forms the basis for large group communication, as every large group is usually socially divided into smaller groups, or parts within the whole.

Large Group Communication

Also called Public Communication, large group communication is a general description of organizational communication as a communication context describing large numbers of individuals who are members of the group. This type of communication usually involves one individual addressing a large gathering of people. Election campaigns and public speeches are examples of this type of communication.

In such cases, there is usually a single sender of information and several receivers who are being addressed. This type of communication is also crucial in establishing a business brand or a professional as an expert, especially in the cases of making presentations or public speaking. In such situations, there still exists the need for clarity, brevity, and impact.

But there is also the need to captivate. One's success with a large group depends on the connection one makes with them. One might have a super slick presentation ready to go, but unless one's audience buys into one's personal brand, the call to action would be easily forgotten.

Verbal communication is, in many ways, very much part of the fabric of any society, and as such, it is crucial for every member of the society to have a good knowledge of verbal communication and the mechanisms that make it work. One important mechanism of note is that the effectiveness of verbal communication depends on the tone of the speaker, clarity of speech, volume, speed, body language and the quality of words used in the conversation.

The workplace is a sector where excellent communication is required. The hallmark of a great leader includes being able to understand his subordinates and communicate to them what is expected to be done. Board meetings, presentations, business pitches and so on are expected to be communicated concisely, without causing confusion for the listeners. Many times, the staff of a company may only be able to send written notes to their superiors. But it has been found that in a workplace where verbal communication is encouraged and everyone is given access to engage in face to face conversations with any other member of the staff, things move in a smoother fashion and the fire of workplace conflicts is easily put out.

In institutions of learning, from the primary to the university level, effective verbal communication is required to impart knowledge. It is imperative that the students are clearly taught using simple words that do not confuse. When there are conflicts or dissatisfactions, a quick meeting where the head addresses the school community always calms things.

In the home, parents are able to understand their kids better when they encourage them to talk. And the children are less confused when they are able to receive clear words from their parents. Siblings are able to build their relationships through efficient communication.

Even verbal communication can be muffled or jumbled. Many people have not mastered the art of communicating the right way. While they might have something to say, they do so in highly confusing ways, using unnecessary terms. Sometimes, their choice of words come off as boring or bland. Combined with the use of nonverbal communication, nobody wants to listen to them. This is why it does not matter one bit how great a person's ideas are. If he is not able to communicate with the right people, it is all pointless.

Why is it important to be able to analyze verbal communication? Simply, in order to avoid conflicts, misunderstandings, and confusion, everyone should be able to correctly grasp and analyze what someone else is saying. That is why it is important for the speaker to string the right words at the right time.

Elements of Verbal Communication

1. Tone: The tone of a person's voice is an important element that conveys a special meaning to the listener. It can be detected from the tone if a person is being rude. Other tone descriptions are cheerful, sad, angry, hurt, surprised, skeptical or bitter. At that, it does not matter so much what the person has said, it is their tone that is measured and used to judge their intentions.

This is why it is important to always adopt the right tone, for, in verbal communication, words are not the only things that are considered. Some people consider some tones to be quite childish. At other times the cadences are perceived as brash, unrefined, and rough. For example, the different tones of saying, "That's my seat" will mean different things.

If the speaker uses a sharp tone, it reveals territoriality and a no-nonsense intention. In another tone, it can mean simple information being passed across to let someone else know that that's where he has been sitting. The speakers have said the same things, but by their use of different tones, they have conveyed different meanings.

2. Voice Speed: The speed with which a person speaks can also be interpreted differently. Slow speaking is often taken to mean that the speaker is sad, depressed, or sluggish, while fast modes show excitement, happiness, or surprise. The words, "I'm glad I am alive," when said slowly, may not be very convincing. The listener may believe the person is really sad being alive but is only trying to feel cheerful. When said fast, the words are convincing, as a person who is glad to be alive is expected to be bubbling with life. The voice speed, therefore, is a highly important consideration when analyzing verbal communication.

3. Language: Of course, speaking a language that a listener does not understand is absolutely pointless. The choice of language involves common sense. Once a person does not understand the language being spoken, verbal communication becomes impossible and the parties involved will have to adopt another means of communicating with each other.

The usefulness of an official language is obvious here. The official language is learned compulsorily in schools of different countries so that when they have cause to come together through immigration, emigration, a business activity, religious activity, sports or education, the language barrier will be broken by using the official language to communicate with all parties.

4. Grammar: Even when the right language is used, the grammar must be proper. Wrong grammar puts listeners off. Nobody wants to listen to disjointed sentences, a low-quality string of words, or get confused because a person is saying "chased" when they meant to say "chaste", or "sanity" when they meant "sanitary". The wrong vocabulary is confusing, makes listening cumbersome for the audience, and ultimately makes them lose interest in the topic, regardless of how important the topic is.

5. The volume of voice: The volume of the speaking voice is also a determinant of how the spoken words will be analyzed. A high volume is typical of sanguines and choleric. They usually have a lot of energy at different times of the day and can command people's attention with their loud and jovial volumes.

Their high volumes reflect happiness, excitement, and fun. Low volumes can command secrecy. The speaker is viewed as interested in communicating with only the physically closest people to him. Thus, it is highly irritating when in a large group, a speaker uses low volume such that people have to strain their ears to grasp what is being said. This is seen a lot of times in universities where there are hundreds of students attending a course.

The lecturer, in the absence of a public address system, becomes defiant, claims he cannot trouble himself and goes ahead to teach only those physically close to him. The rest of the students dig in their heels and lose interest in the lecture. In the same vein, it is unseemly for a person with an audience of one to speak with a very high volume. The audience will end up getting startled continually, and their ears may hurt. Eventually, they will have to tell the speaker to reduce his voice.

These elements are critical during an analysis of verbal communication. Everyone should be able to process what has been said to them. When a listener is not able to understand what is being said, the goal of the communication is lost and no desired results are achieved. In the different sectors of life and business, people should be taught to communicate properly and listeners should be taught to listen carefully and ask questions where they are not clear.

There are various means by which people can be trained to do this. In order to improve the ability to analyze the verbal communication, the following practical exercises can be adopted. Some of the exercises are in forms of games. While games are perceived by some as childish, they are some of the best ways to teach important topics because games engage the full concentration of a person.

They are thus able to learn fast what the principles they require are, especially when there's a stake of winning or losing. This book will recommend games and other practical activities that help to improve the ability to analyze verbal communication.

Exercise 1: Rumor Monger

This is a game that can be played by a group of ten or more people. In the workplace where coworkers are being taught the analysis of verbal communication, for example, the staff can be organized in groups. The head of the group will say a short sentence or phrase into the ear of one of the group members only once. The hearer will not be permitted to ask for a repeat of said words. He or she will then go on and tell another member of the group whatever they heard.

The next person will do the same and the next person too until all the members of the group have received the passed down information. The last person to receive the information will tell everyone what he or she heard. Mostly, whatever the last person says will result in the laughter of the entire house as it will be totally different from what was originally told the first member of the group by the group head.

This game reflects how easy it is to spread something untrue just because one person heard the wrong thing and did not confirm the authenticity of what they have heard. It impresses upon the audience and game volunteers how important it is to confirm whatever they hear from the very source, and how they shouldn't tell someone else what they know may not be authentic.

Exercise 2: Role Playing

In order to improve verbal communication analysis, either interpersonal or group, role-playing is highly practical in understanding how. This exercise involves groups of twos or threes. They pretend to be one thing while the other group pretends to be another. If this exercise is being used in the workplace, say among members of a restaurant staff, two or three of them can pretend to be customers.

One of them may pretend to order for a rare dish which involves the waiter having to understand exactly what the customer is asking for. Another of the members can pretend to be a dissatisfied customer who has come to lodge a complaint in person, and another can be making a home delivery order and putting down his address. The other group can then pretend to be waiters, managers, customer care workers, and delivery persons.

This activity will help them feel in the shoes of the customers they deal with every day and they'd learn to listen more carefully to them in the future by analyzing their speeches without making mistakes that can be costly to the business. This activity can be used in various business sectors, home settings, schools and so on.

Exercise 3: Book Rotation

Books are good old friends that seem to solve every problem. In order to gain understanding, reading is recommended. In the workplace, the manager can select a particular book that helps improve the analysis of verbal communication. This book is then rotated among coworkers, allocating an equal amount of reading time for each of the readers. After everyone has read the book, a discussion time can be scheduled where everyone tells what they have learned from the book and how they hope to use it to improve their analysis of personal and group verbal communications.

Exercise 4: Simple Yes or No

The simple yes or no activity is designed to help people learn to be concise in their speeches. A group of twos is needed at a time to practice this activity. One person asks the other a question to which they are only expected to answer yes or no. Additional words are regarded as needless and may disqualify the member. It has been found that some overly complicated speeches confuse people needlessly. Most times, a simple yes or no will answer the question.

Example:

- **Question**: The weather is really mild today, don't you think so, Fred?
- **Simple answer**: No, I don't think so, sir.
- **Complicated Answer**: The weather has been fluctuating a lot this week.

Example:

- **Question**: Is Clara dead or alive?
- **Simple answer**: Yes, she is dead.
- **Complicated answer**: She's temporarily transferred to another state of entropy that does not let her feel alive.

The best orators have been found to make use of simple speeches, making sure that everyone in the room can understand them when they speak. This is good verbal communication.

Exercise 5: Building Game

This game can also be used to foster good verbal communication among people working together in a team. The team is divided into three groups with about three members in each group. The first group makes use of building blocks of different colors to construct a little house. The second group then goes to see the house and takes an accurate description of the house to the third group verbally. The third group builds according to what the second group verbally describes to them. In the end, the three groups come together to see if the work of the third group is in any way similar to that of the original builders'. Wrong communication or wrong analysis of communication will lead the third group to build the wrong structure. The three groups can rotate their roles to grant every member the privilege to be a part of all the three groups involved in the game.

Exercise 6: Listening Activity

Nothing beats training up the ability to listen correctly in an effort to improve the ability to analyze verbal communication. Listening is a very important part of communication. This is different from hearing. Hearing is the ability to grasp the words with the appropriate organs. Listening involves much more than that. Listening engages the mind, it involves accurate processing, and the avoidance of misjudgment.

A person who has not learned to listen will usually interpret spoken words in the wrong way. Let the members of the team put down words from audio onto a notepad. The audio can be three or four minutes long. Play the audio about three or four times to the group. Then ask them to write down what points the speaker was trying to make and what they feel the audio is all about.

The game can also be played in another form. Let each of the group members have a headset on and play the audio by themselves. Let them transcribe accurately, word for word, the speeches in the audio.

The head of the group should review every submitted answer for accuracy. This activity should be repeated as often as possible to help the learners improve their verbal communication analysis skills, thus making the workplace or home a better place for all.

Exercise 7: Blindfolding

The blindfolding game is multi-efficient, but it can also be used in improving verbal communication skill analysis of people. The team of learners is divided into two groups. Two volunteers from each group are selected and blindfolded. They are then told to go get something across the room. Since they cannot see, they are able to avoid going the wrong way or colliding with objects in the room by listening to the directions given by their other team members. If they are not able to accurately interpret the instructions of their team members, they will not be able to attain their goals.

Simple as some of these activities may sound, they are reflections of what happens to us every day. Misinterpretation of the instructions given by the general manager to the human resource manager can lead the human resource manager to do things that will cost the organization to lose a lot of money.

Children not understanding what their parents are trying to say can result in rebellion and resentment, ultimately breaking the family. A teacher may feel insulted at what a student says because he misinterpreted the student's words. It's in the same way that siblings can misunderstand each other and become sworn enemies. Two nations can go to war simply because of a verbal misunderstanding that resulted from one of the parties wrongly analyzing what has been said.

We must note that body language also plays a key role in effective communication. Even while verbal communication is being used, if the body language does not match what is being said or any of the elements of voice tone, volume, language, grammar, and voice speed are not aligned, the speaker can still take what has been said to mean another thing entirely.

The stakes are too high to make mistakes while analyzing the verbal communication in our day to day activities. It is important that we have an accurate understanding, and that we keep improving. That way, there's a gross reduction in conflicts that may arise from wrong analysis during verbal communication.

Chapter 2: Practical Exercises To Read Body Language

It is important that you learn how to understand body language. But before then you should know in what areas of body language you're lacking.

1. Establish eye contact: Whenever you're talking to other people, try to make direct eye contact. When you do that, you're letting the person know that you have an interest in what they are talking about. If you have to give a presentation at work then you will need to make eye contact with your audience. Because of this, they will know that you have confidence in the topic you're presenting. Also, when you make eye contact with people, they feel comfortable enough to continue the conversation with you. But then, be careful with how much you look at people as they will be uncomfortable if your eye contact turns into a stare.

2. Use your facial expressions: Let your facial expressions carry your emotions. The message expressed by facial expressions is largely universal and that means they mean the same thing everywhere. Anywhere you meet a frowning person, then the person is upset.

Use smiles in your conversation as long as it is not regarded as inappropriate for the situation. That way, people will know that you are happy and not in a bad mood. The atmosphere for the conversation will also be warm and friendly and others will be comfortable. Because of how well your face displays emotions, be careful not to make unpleasant faces when smiles are not needed. When you show a look of seriousness in a formal setting, it means that you are engaged with the present situation.

3. Consider personal space: Notice your proximity to other people. People have different ways of viewing proximity so it is important for you to observe if the person you're communicating with is uncomfortable. This means that you're standing somewhat too close and that they would need some distance between you two. You can express emotions by the amount of physical space you give.

4. Mind your posture: Observe your posture. If you slouch, it means that you have no interest in what a person says. The way your body moves is important.

When you swing your legs during a meeting, you're showing how bored, impatient, and uninterested you are. Face the others and sit up straight when you are talking or listening.

5. Observe tones and sounds: The sounds and tone of voice that you use can express your thoughts to people even when you don't say a word. If you receive directions from a manager and grunt immediately, your manager is getting the signal that you disapprove of what they say. The tone you use can make people know that you're angry, frustrated, or sarcastic. Speak softly and try not to sigh too often or talk in a high pitched tone.

So, what if you've discovered which of the above areas of body language you're lacking? You will need to work on them to improve using some practical exercises. These exercises are often used to encourage team building in different settings like sports teams, schools, performing arts groups, workplaces, and religious organizations. The time frame of the activities can vary. Some are just two-minute exercises, while some last longer and could take up to several weeks or days.

These activities are chosen because the participants can do them silently and in addition to improving their ability to detect nonverbal cues, they will build their communication skills and trust.

During nonverbal communication, if both parties do not understand the body signs used then misunderstandings can occur. These exercises were created to help people understand what nonverbal communication stands for and how important it is. While communicating non-verbally, it is important for both parties to understand the cues to avoid any kind of misunderstandings. These are some of the activities that one can engage in with other adults to learn about nonverbal communication:

Exercise 1: Eye-Spot

This exercise seeks to improve your ability to spot details. First, you will watch a short video clip of any chosen character and proceed to point out all the body language gestures that make up the character's personality. Do you notice how he/she shows comfort and/or discomfort? Notice if the person has open/closed body language. For better effect, the group should watch the video clip first without using the sound and then participants can state what they think the dialogue is about. After that, the video clip should be played with sounds and all the predictions should be evaluated. Did the gestures and the words used match?

Exercise 2: A Sticky Situation

All participants should pull out a sheet and pen down a "sticky situation". They could describe characters facing challenges like being pulled over by the police, finding out they possess magical powers, or hearing that they have only 3 weeks to live. Gather the situations described.

When the class starts, pick up one situation and ask the students to devote 5 minutes to write how they imagine their character will react. Review the answers as a class and let the participants point out the gestures that their character shows. This activity can help the participants learn more about the characters.

Exercise 3: Actions Are Louder Than Words

Let's say the character you chose has just been delivered a postcard from someone they have not heard from in a long while. Supply the reader with two sentences that show the content of the letter and then use the remaining time to demonstrate how the character acts when looking, reading, and dropping the letter. Concentrate on body language.

You should not forget that the body language expressed by the character is supposed to tell us more than their words.

Exercise 4: The World As Your Character Knows It

The participants can do this activity as a writing assignment or as a role play. There are two ways of conducting it:

1. The character while watching television is drawn to the current event and/or topic. What is their response?

2. The character then appears in that time period and/or setting. What does your character see? Explain it with the details they have learned. Emphasize the reactions given off by the character through their thoughts, dialogue, actions.

Exercise 5: A Not-So-Normal Encounter

If two of the characters created by the group should meet for the first time, what would happen? Let two participants come to the front of the group and role play these characters. Let one of the participants create the setting that they will meet in. It could be a party, the bus station, red light, church, etc.

Let each participant give the group an overview of their character for about 30 seconds. The participants will role-play for two minutes and while at it, they will concentrate on the dialogue and body language. Let the group answer questions and decide if the dialogue and body language looked real enough for the characters.

Exercise 6: Gesture List

The participants should be able to answer questions like, "How do we communicate without using words?" and, "Which gestures are commonly used?" The participants should be divided into groups and each group should be able to show as many ways of communicating nonverbally as they can in 1 minute (eg: shrug, shake the head, make a face, hands-on-hips, wink, smile, finger to lips, nod head).

Exercise 7: Silent Scene

The participants should form pairs. Each pair should create a one minute scene that happens in one location. Let the pairs have a problem that requires solving. Nobody in the scene should be allowed to talk. Any communication that needs to be made should be nonverbal. The audience should look on and try to guess what is being acted in the scene without having any dialogue as a guide. The participants can refer to the gestures list.

Exercise 8: Nonverbal Communication

The participants should be provided with a list of sentences and then they should try to communicate them nonverbally. The students can also refer to the gesture list.

Exercise 9: Nonverbal Emotions

Participants can select an emotion by pulling slips of paper from a hat. They should present whatever emotion they find written on the slip of paper in a wordless performance. Space should be carved out where they can enter, sit, stand up and exit the space. The intention is to "show" that emotion very well so that the audience can guess (emotions can be disgust, happiness, anger, sadness, boredom, fear, excitement, stress, etc).

Exercise 10: Nonverbal Picture Prompt

Let the participants see a picture of a person. What are they communicating with their body language? The participant should create an inner monologue for this character.

Exercise 11: High Status/Low Status

The participants should walk around the room and try to physically understand what a high status and low status means. What makes a high-status body? What makes a low-status body? How is their walking posture? What is the relationship between this physicality and the way they interact? Participants should be grouped into pairs of one high-status character and one low-status character. The pair is required to present a nonverbal scene that indicates their status.

Exercise 12: Subtext Scene

The participants should form groups. Let them act out a scene where one character is presented with lines that say one thing but their body language is showing another thing. For instance, a participant tells another participant that they are happy that they passed an exam while their body language is rigid and their arms are folded across their body.

Exercise 13: Good Listener/Bad Listener

Two participants should volunteer to stand in front. Person A should tell Person B a story. For the first time, Person B is a good listener. Let the rest of the participants state what a good listener looks like. How can engagement be communicated nonverbally? The scene should be repeated. This time Person B will tell the story while Person A will listen. Person A will portray a bad listener.

The audience should focus on two people. How does a bad listener appear? How can you communicate boredom without words? The audience should indicate if they can see the difference.

Exercise 14: One Talker/One Not

The participants should form pairs. Let each pair act out a one-minute scene that occurs in one location with a problem that should be solved. The first person, Person A, should speak their lines while Person B should reply only with the use of gestures, body language, and other forms of nonverbal communication. When the time elapses, they should both switch sides and Person A should be the nonverbal communicator.

Exercise 15: Judging

The participants should answer these questions: Have you ever judged someone by their appearance or the way they move before you talk to them? What part of a person's physicality affects you? Let the participants create a scene. The characters in the scene should be judged by the nonverbal communication that they use and not their words.

Exercise 16: Lining Up

The participants should be given instruction that they have just two minutes to form a line in a certain order without having to talk or make any sound. Another instruction will be given to them where they have to line up based on certain criteria. It could be by height, shoe size, alphabetically by the first name, or even by shirt color. The leader should make the instructions a little vague and allow the participants to choose by themselves how to use the given criteria and the formation of the line.

For instance, if the leader instructs them to line up by hair color, the participants should be left with the decision of choosing the order of arrangement of the colors. The participants can repeat the exercise as many times as they want. This exercise will help people to learn how to make decisions, take up leadership and organizational roles and work as a team even with nonverbal communications.

Exercise 17: Designing Together

The participants will divide themselves into teams consisting of four to six people each. The teams are each provided with a brown paper bag containing objects like small building blocks, clay, paper clips, pine cones, plastic silverware, toothpicks, paper cups, coins, and rubber bands.

A flip chart is also provided for each of the teams. They are then required to make use of the items in their bags as materials to design a product. They'd use them to also make a flier that tells the name of the product and advertise it. While doing all these, they should not speak or write notes to each other. The team members can use this method to practice nonverbal communication skills, feedback methods, body language skills, and creativity.

Exercise 18: Improv. Scene

Some of these activities are coined from drama games and improvisation techniques. This improv scene activity is among the drama related activities. It involves getting a group of people to act in a silent scene. The actors here are not pretending to talk like in charades. Instead, they are acting out a scene where the people communicate silently. The scene can be set in a library, a room with a sleeping baby, or a reading room.

Exercise 19: Mirrors

This activity is also a drama warm-up that fits easily for people wanting to improve their team-building skills. The participants are grouped in pairs or everyone stands in a circle. The leader then makes slow movements with some body parts like the head, arms, body, and hands. The other people in the circle will try to copy her actions exactly. To make this exercise work, the participants are to follow the leader without hesitation. They should endeavor to time their actions so they are as close as possible. They would form a mirror image so that it is hard to differentiate who the leader is and who the followers are. The leader, however, should try to use body movements that will be easy to imitate. The leader can also use eye contact to show the next move.

Exercise 20: Charades

With charades, you will understand that nonverbal communication can be used to communicate very complex ideas without having to use words. The participants can play a game of charades. However, it will be better to dump the TV shows and musical artists for normal messages and emotions used every day like, "I don't know how to operate a computer." Using everyday messages will make the activity more practical.

Exercise 21: Photo Interpretations

You can also learn about nonverbal communication by directly analyzing it. The participants will form groups to study and interpret photos of people who are using nonverbal means to express their emotions, character, and feelings. When the participants look at them, they should be able to see a lot from them. After the participants identify the emotions they see from the pictures individually, the discussion should be opened to everybody in the group and the participants can then try to check for disagreements or confirm that the nonverbal communication was clear to all.

Exercise 22: Guess The Movie Game

The participants should be divided into two teams. One team should come up with a movie and tell it to a member of the other team. The person who was told the movie title has to come out in front of all and either act out the movie title or some of the movie scenes in a way that their team will recognize what movie it is.

If the team can recognize the movie, then it becomes the turn of the first team to send a member to the next team to get the name of a movie for them. Then they will guess the movie title after their member demonstrates. The cycle is repeated—one member from one team goes to the other to listen and act out a movie while their team members are faced with the task of recognizing.

Exercise 23: Opposite expressions

One participant will be provided with a script. They must then read the contents of the script but replace all the emotions expressed in the dialogs with opposite emotions. Let's say the script states that the person should laugh. Instead of laughing, the person will read out the dialog with angry or sad expressions.

This game is regarded as a nonverbal game despite having to use words because the description is based on moods and expressions. If a person can properly read gestures, expressions, and other people's moods then they will do well in the game.

Exercise 24: Paper Strip Acting

Paper strips should be made and shared equally in two. A dialog should be written on one set of paper strips and kept in a bowl. The next set of paper strips should carry moods or disposition and they should be kept in another bowl. Every participant should get one paper strip from each of the two bowls so they can serve as prompts. They will first read out the dialog in front and also read the mood written on the other slip. After that, they have to read it without making any expression.

The role of the audience will be to guess what mood the dialog was read in and note it down. Although it involves speaking, this game is regarded as nonverbal because you have to recognize moods and expressions.

Exercise 25: Make A Silent Movie

The participants will have to be shared into groups. They would perform the task of writing out screenplays for a silent movie and give out the roles to actors. The actors must then act out the script without using words. All groups get to participate in the performance and also watch the others acting.

Exercise 26: Follow The Leader

The participants will select one person to be their leader. Then the leader makes signs that others follow, while the rest of the people follow the leader's signals without talking either. Anybody who makes a mistake will be disqualified and will have to quit the game. After every turn, new leaders will be chosen. The first leader will pick someone else to take over using only gestures. The game will go on until there's only one person left as the winner.

Exercise 27: Draw And Explain

The participants should divide themselves into groups. Every group has to draw something. The next team then makes an effort to interpret the drawing and what it is supposed to mean. The groups take turns at drawing and interpreting the work of others.

Exercise 28: Introduce Your Friend

Everybody in the group has to find someone to pair with. They will both introduce themselves to each other and say their names without letting others know.

When everybody is done getting acquainted, a pair will stand in front of every other person and make an attempt to introduce their partner to the audience without words. When they do that, the other participants will guess the name of the person.

Exercise 29: Catching a Chicken

Four participants should volunteer to leave the room. Notify the volunteers to come in at once, after you have told them to show the audience how to catch a chicken.

Each volunteer should be called upon one after the other to perform this task. The person who volunteers last will guess what actions they think the others were performing. The second to the last volunteer will say his thoughts and the second person will follow suit. After that, the first person will have to come out and say what he was doing.

Exercise 30: Guess Dialogs From a Silent Movie

Let the group watch a silent film. Then select some individuals to come out and show everyone what they think could be the dialogue of the movie. The audience will be the judge and decide if it's good.

Exercise 31: Copycat

Tell everybody to stand in a circle. Let somebody volunteer to go out for a minute. Let a leader be chosen unanimously without using words, only nonverbal cues. The leader will keep switching actions without informing the volunteer that they are leading. The participants will then follow and copy the actions of the leader. The members have to follow and copy the leader without making it obvious. The volunteer has to stand in the middle of the circle and try to find out who the leader is. If they succeed in finding out the leader, then they win.

Exercise 32: Wireless Communication

Somebody in the group should place a rope on the ground. After that, they are to select a listener. The listener should be brought 20 feet forward and blindfolded. This person will not say any word throughout the game and will also not move unless instructed to do so. The group will have to select a communicator. The person should be brought 10 feet forward and turned until they face the group. They have to stand on the starting line. When the communicator is positioned, they may or may not turn around to face the listener. Throughout the game, the communicator is the only person permitted to speak.

A set of instructions should be created for the group using props. For instance, "Instruct the listener to tie the scarf around their head, the glove should be worn and they should pull off their shoe." The communicator will get information from the group silently to pass on to the blindfolded listener.

Exercise 33: Alphabetically

In this activity, the group is told to call out the letters of the alphabet in order. No two participants are meant to say the same letter at once. The participants can choose any sequence they want apart from ones like holidays, numbers, and months.

Exercise 34: Jedi Mind Trick

The participants should be made to stand in a circle with someone in the middle. Everybody is expected to remain silent. The person in the middle will try to take the place of one person in the circle. Those in the circle will attempt to exchange places without losing their place to the person in the middle.

To achieve their goals, the participants will have to communicate and negotiate their moves using eye contact and nonverbal cues.

Exercise 35: Human Knot

The participants of the group should entangle their limbs and try to loosen them. The group should be shared into two smaller teams if the participants are many.

The two groups should sit in a tight circle stretch out their arms and hold a person who is seated beside them but not directly. The tangling can take place at any speed that suits the participants. But, the detangling should be done with care to avoid causing injury to anybody. The participants should avoid speaking while they carry out the activity and instead they should use gestures.

Exercise 36: Group Drawing

The group should be shared into teams. Each team will have to collaborate and make drawings based on a particular idea or theme. There should be a five-second limit after which one person will pass the drawing onto the next person to make their own contribution to it. All communications should be made using cues. Every person has to contribute to the drawing. Another image should be selected and this time it should be passed round in a different order than the first.

To make it even more fun, the teams can be asked to switch their unfinished pictures or exchange artists when they are halfway through the activity.

Chapter 3: Practical Exercises To Persuade People

Persuasion is a phenomenon that is never easy at all. Some people are just blessed with the gift of persuasion, meaning that they can get people to do what they want with as little stress as possible. Keep it in mind that the people that do this also find it hard to persuade other difficult sets of people when the time comes. Then there is a group of people that have no experience at all when it comes to persuasion. They are the kind of people that could not persuade a person to save their lives.

Persuasion is a skill that everyone should have because it has a way of making people feel more in control of the things that go on around them. If you are part of the group that has little or no idea how to persuade people effectively or you are part of the group that knows how to but still wants to brush up on your game, there are certain things you need to try in order to get what you want almost every time through the art of persuasion. These skills would show their full effectiveness when it is practiced over and over again. Here are some exercises to try:

Exercise 1: Dress The Part At All Times

First impressions mean everything. This is why you must never slip up when it comes to looking your best at all times. When you walk into a room, especially when it is a room where you want to convince a person or a group of people, make sure that you make them understand that you mean business and that you are not there for jokes through your dressing. You can't walk into a room with people that are properly dressed and you look like a car ran your clothes over and expect to get their attention in any way. That is almost impossible.

When you get into the venue where you are supposed to persuade the person (or people), make sure that your dressing emits confidence before you say hello to the client or group of clients. When you can successfully achieve that, there is a huge possibility that you would be able to persuade them to do what you think is best for them.

This is the reason why you will see real estate agents dressing so professionally and so clean. They want to pass the message across that they know what is best for you, and if you have fallen for something like that in the past, you might have been successfully persuaded. This is why dressing the part is important. You must know that dressing the part when you want to persuade someone to do something can be the difference between getting what you want and missing out on a huge deal. In order to get what you want, look the part first and watch every other thing fall in place.

Dressing the part is good and all, but there are some things that you must never do when you dress to impress. Some of those things include:

A. **Never dress inappropriately**: This is the last thing you want to do when you tend to dress to look the part. When you want your clothes to speak for you, you want them to say good and confident things about you, and they can't say those things when they are clothes that show a lot of skin or expose unnecessary parts of your body.

This is something that can throw someone off their game immediately. Some people may say nothing about it when they see you because they want to be polite, and they do not want to feel like they are intruding in your personal life, but deep down, they have lost all respect for you. Those kinds of people might not even call you to do anything for them again in the future. There are a lot of ways dressing inappropriately can be bad for you.

Take, for instance, if you are a real estate agent and you want to show a couple a house that you want them to buy and you dress like you came to seduce someone. There is no way that couple is buying that house, especially if one of them feels like you are trying to seduce their spouse whether male or female. Learn to wear clothes that do not say negative things about you, whether true or false.

You should learn to wear clothes that only say good things about you. Clothes that will get the attention of the person you are trying to convince in a positive way. When you successfully establish that, you have gotten half your problems covered.

B. **Never be overconfident**: A lot of people get this part wrong all the time, whether they are trying to convince someone or not. When you dress well, you mustn't make every other person around you feel inferior in any way. You may look at yourself right now and think, "I don't do that," but there is a chance that you do but do not notice because you are so used to it already. You probably see it as practically nothing anymore.

If you want to know if you are this kind of person, ask a friend that would not lie to you and see what they have to say. Some people tend to be overconfident immediately when they notice that they are better dressed than you are. It's as if, upon finding out they look better than everyone, their clothes send a signal to their minds that boosts their confidence. Such people would go into a place where they are supposed to persuade someone to get something, only to get distracted as they start to slightly comment on the other person's dressing. The manner in which they do so would often seem insulting, even though they have no such intentions.

You do not want the person you are trying to persuade to think that you are in any way trying to insult or put them down. This is because when they start to think like that, your chances of ever convincing them to do anything drop to almost zero. There are stories of people that walk out of a meeting simply because of what someone said about their attire.

If you are able to avoid these two things when you dress to impress, there is absolutely no way that you are going to fail in persuading a person or a group of people. That is, if you have the right skills, of course, because dressing the right way is not the only way you can get what you want out of a person. There are a lot of other ways.

Exercise 2: Use The Right Words Every Time

As humans, we are bound to make some mistakes when we talk, especially when we are nervous, but this is a slip up that you do not want when you are trying to convince a person to do something.

When you are talking with the person you are trying to convince, it is important that you speak to them with powerful words. Words that are not only going to get their attention, but also keep their attention on you. One of the main aims of persuading a person is to make them agree with what you want them to do, no matter how absurd it may be. This would not be possible if you do not know how to talk to them.

One of the key factors of persuasion is good communication in any form, but you also need to back them up with powerful words that would put excitement in their minds and would also intrigue them to know more. There are a lot of people that go to school for years and years so that they would be able to talk to people and get them to do virtually anything that they want them to do.

These kinds of people use different methods to be able to talk to their clients at all times, but you should know that the professionals hardly use one method twice on the same client, especially if that client just had an encounter with them. They try to switch things up a bit. This tip does not only work in the business sector, but it could also work in the home.

If you know the right words to say to your dad, words that would be able to persuade and convince him at the same time, you would be able to get what you want and when you want it without much stress at all. All you have to do is find words that relate to the particular person that you are trying to persuade, and when you have that, there is a good chance that you would be able to persuade them.

Good professionals go into a conversation with a person that they are trying to convince without any form of preparation in the form of what to say. They come up with what they want to say as they go.

To convince someone, it is expected that you would have studied the person and memorized the words to use. But if you think you won't be able to remember them, you could use cue cards. However, this might make your persuasive abilities unconvincing. It is important that you hide the cards away from the person you are trying to convince the best you can.

If you won't be able to use the cards and successfully hide them at the same time, you could use certain trigger words. Trigger words are those words that can be used to help remember certain power words that you want to use on someone. For instance, if you are trying to pitch an idea of a safer car to a person and your power word is "accidents," and you feel like you are going to forget it, you could use the word "collision" to remember it.

This whole process may sound and look like a lot of work, but it is a technique that has been known to help a lot of people get to where they are now in the art of persuasion. Talking to a person the right way and using the words that you know that the person would be able to relate to is just you getting one step closer to persuading them. In a scenario when you have two or more people in a room to persuade, you have to change things up a bit because there is no way that the power word you are using on a particular person would apply to the rest of the people.

So what do you do? You have to think on your feet. When you get into the room, try and use different power words to get everyone's attention at the same time. It is not compulsory that you must get the attention of everyone there, but you must be able to get the attention of the majority of them because if you successfully do that, the others would have no other choice but to sit down and listen to what it is you have to say.

Making power words is not as easy as it sounds, but there are some power words that you would be able to use on people to get their attention and hold their attention till you are done with the persuasion. Some of these words include:

- **Because**: "Because" is a word that is used to show the reason for something or why that particular event occurred. If you are going to use any power word when you try and persuade someone, "because" is the word for you. This does not mean that you should start and end every sentence with it, because that would be downright absurd and annoying.

  When you use "because", it should be when you are trying to convince them of why they should get something or why they shouldn't. For instance, you could say that "you should get a new car because the old one does not have an airbag and it could be very dangerous in the event of an accident."

  No one would listen to you when you tell them to get or do something when they do not know the reason why they are supposed to get or do it. When you use the word because, you could try and increase the pitch of your voice so that they would be alert at all times, especially when you use the word. If you use this word the way you are supposed to, you don't need to talk much when it comes to persuading a person.

All you have to do is to tell them that they need to get something and tell them why they need to get it, and if you play your cards right, you might have successfully persuaded a person without stressing yourself. This would also work if you are a teenager and you are trying to convince your parents to get you a new phone. When you go to them, tell them that you need a new phone and before they start shooting your planes of ideas down, start telling them why you need it.

This is why it is important to practice what you are going to say and how you are going to say it. If you pitch your reasons very well and they like it, you are definitely getting a new phone, but if they don't, you could always try and try again.

- **You**: When you use the word "you" when you are trying to persuade someone, it helps the person focus more on you and less on anything or anyone around them. For instance, if you were talking to a person and you were trying to persuade him or her, and you said, "You sir, doesn't that sound nice?" The person's focus would turn to you at that time because you succeeded in engaging him or her in what you were doing.

One of the main reasons why people lose focus or attention during conversations like that is because they get bored, but if you succeed in engaging them in the conversation, there is a huge chance that their attention would be yours to do whatever you want to do with. "You" can also be effective when you are trying to pass a message across to a larger group of people. When you are trying to persuade a group of people to do something, you could call out a person from time to time to ask his or her opinion on what you have been saying.

This means that you are engaging the crowd, and no one knows who is next, so they would want to listen so that if you call on them, they would be able to pitch in just like everyone else. This can also help you because when you are trying to interact with the people, you hear their opinions, which makes persuading them even easier. If you know who you want to persuade, it would not be hard for you to get what you want from them.

This word is also used in schools a lot, especially with students that do not interact in class. When you engage them every time and call them out by saying the word "you" when you are supposed to, there is a chance that you are going to go places in terms of persuasion.

- **Free**: This is a word that does not sound like it has any power at all, but the word "free" is more powerful than you could ever imagine. One thing people love the most in the world is free stuff. Sometimes these people do not even care what the stuff is as far as it is free; they are going to take it. If you want to pitch an idea to someone, especially when it comes to the person buying something, and you add freebies to the deal, statistics show that they would take the offer before you've completed the sentence.

Some people would even bring some friends and family members to see the beautiful deal that you had planned for them simply because you talked to them and used the word "free" when you were trying to persuade them. Sometimes, you do not need to throw in a free deal for you to get their attention at all. You could try getting some stuff around like free chocolates, free refreshments, or free snacks.

This is why you would see that on certain occasions when people get tired and want to go home, the host comes out and says that there will be free refreshments at the end of the occasion. Upon hearing that, a lot of people would stay back even when they are exhausted. That shows you how powerful the word free is.

These words are not the only powerful persuading words about there. There are still hundreds more, but you should know that none of them would effectively work for you when you do not know how to use them. There is a huge possibility that you use these words almost every single day, but the reason why you have not noticed it is that you are not using the words in the right way and in the right scenario. If you want your power words to create an impact anytime you use them, then use them properly.

Exercise 3: Do Not Force It

You should never look desperate to the person you are trying to convince. You could be very desperate, but the last thing you want to do is to show that desperation on your face because if you do, they would waste no time in taking advantage of you. When you have pitched the idea to them once or twice in a week or month, make yourself scarce to them for as long as you possibly can. That is, after telling them that what you are offering them is a limited time offer and it's been pursued by a lot of people even if it has not.

There are a lot of people out there, whether they are into business or not, that want what everyone wants. When you let them know that the offer you are placing on the table is under limited time, there is a huge possibility that they would want that offer as quickly as possible, which means that you are persuading them even without being in front of them.

If you want this technique to work, you mustn't check upon them all the time, and if you guys meet in person, you could pretend to talk to another person that needs that same offer, and when they see that you mean business, there is no way that they are going to be wasting more time.

Before you know it, you have persuaded them by staying away from them. This can also be done with a lot of people as well. The thing is that it is said to be more effective with a group of people because when a group of people are pitched a juicy idea, and they are all aware of the fact that the idea is under limited time, they would want to get it over with as soon as possible. Some of them would even want to finalize the deal there and then.

The trick here is to play your cards right and don't let anyone call your bluff at all. If they try to make you flinch and bring out the desperate person in you, stay calm because they will come and find you.

If you are going to use this for business oriented purposes and you do not have a lot of clients, it is not advised that you use this method because you may lose your one and only client. The thing with people who are just starting is that the person that you are trying to persuade expects you to be with them all the time. The person also expects you to be available to him or her at all times, especially if they have questions.

This can be successfully achieved by a professional, someone who has been at it for a long time, and someone that already has a lot of clients that know what that person is capable of. When that kind of person is trying to pull this kind of stunt, they would not be questioned in any way because their clients know that you are a professional, and they know that a lot of people want and need your services at all times.

This would work even better when you have a lot of good ratings from a lot of promising clients. When there is only good news going around about you, all you have to do is to set things in motion and watch every other thing fall into place with little or no stress involved.

It is imperative to know that a technique like this can only be done and perfected with a lot of practice and determination. You can have all the clients in the world to persuade but you do not know how to put things like this to your advantage and if you do not practice enough before going into things like this, they would know immediately that you are bluffing and it would not take them long before they devour you.

If you are the type that already has a way of doing things and your clients are used to what you do but take advantage of you, and you want to change things up a bit, you can always do that no matter how strange it may be. The only thing you have to do is to make sure that you do not force it on them.

When you try to employ the new method to the way you persuade them, make sure that you do it at their own pace. Do not rush them to fit in. The last thing you want to do is give the person you are trying to persuade an ultimatum. When you try the new method on the first person, slowly take that method to all the other clients. For instance, if you pitch an idea to a group of people and you tell one privately that the offer is limited, that person would eventually leak the news. Before you know it, people would come for the offer. If you don't rush it, you would be surprised at the outcome.

Exercise 4: Understand Their Language

Understanding their language does not necessarily mean that if the person you are trying to persuade speaks French, you should too. But, it means that you should learn to understand their mannerisms, as it would help you a lot in trying to convince them. How? Everyone would want to do something with people that think like them. People that share their ideas and thoughts at the same time.

If you can let them know that you have their ideas in your head at all times, there is a huge chance that you would be able to pitch virtually any idea to them, and they would listen to you because you think like them. When you understand how a person talks and what the person normally does, it would be easier for you to go to places that other people can't.

Talking about language, you can also try and understand the language of the person you are trying to persuade. It may be French, Spanish, or Italian. This does not mean that you should go to your room and cram the whole French dictionary in one night because if you do that, you are only going to be hurting yourself.

When you want to learn the language of the person you are trying to convince, all you have to do is to learn easy things like how they greet and probably how they say yes or no. For instance, if you are supposed to persuade a Japanese businessperson and you start the meeting with a bow, there is a huge possibility that you have gotten the respect of that person.

In persuasion, the slightest things are known to get you the biggest results, which means that you do not need to do big things like learning the person's full language. All you have to do is to know what to say in their language and what not to. When you can get their attention when you say something in their language, there is a huge possibility that you are going to persuade them effectively.

You should also understand that learning the entire language of a person is not bad at all if you have the time, but if you don't, it is advised that you stick to the basics and let the rest play out for itself. You could also try to use key points and notes when you are talking in their language, but be warned that some people may see it as unprofessional and some other people may see it as good and they may be impressed at the fact that you are going all out to make them feel comfortable.

When you want to learn to speak the language of a person in any way, there are certain things that you should never do. These things could be the difference between you getting what you want, and you get kicked out. These things include:

- **Don't overdo it**: This is something that a lot of people do. Some people can't help themselves to the extent that they start saying things that they don't want to. If you are going to learn the language of a person, stick to the easy stuff because you do not want to bite off more than you can chew.

- **Pronounce your words as clearly as you possibly can**: If you want to impress the person you are trying to convince, you must learn how to pronounce every word the exact way it is. This may seem difficult because most pronunciation requires accents, but if you want to make your presence known, pronounce the words properly. If you do not pronounce the words properly, it may mean something else and may seem offensive to the person you are trying to persuade. You do not want your "hello" to sound like "you're stupid", do you?

  If you try to pronounce the words over and over again and you are not getting it right, you could try using the Internet to get the pronunciation the right way. There are a lot of videos and pictures out there that teach people how to pronounce certain words, including in the English language. When you get acquainted with all these words and pronounce them the way they are supposed to, you would be able to pass a clearer and more vivid message to the person or group of people you are trying to relate to.

- **Do not feel like you know everything**: This could probably be your downfall. If you keep it in mind that you know everything and do not need the help of anyone at all in any way, there is absolutely no way that you are going to be able to learn the language of a person. Learn to ask questions not only from Google. Ask questions to people that know the language, people that have a lot of years of experience. The bottom line is to ask people who do not find it hard to understand the language. The last thing you want to do is to feel like you know everything because if you do, you would just be walking into the lion's den blindly, and you do not want those lions to devour you.

With all of these listed and explained, if you can avoid all these and make sure that you stick to what you need to do, there is a significant chance that you would be able to persuade anyone using their language. If you believe that the language thing is going to be bad for you, you can always abandon that strategy and stick to English. This is because you can speak their language and still fail to convince them.

Exercise 5: Timing Is Everything

Timing is indeed everything when you are trying to convince or persuade a person to do something that you want. When you want to persuade a person, you must do so at specific times. You need to study the person you want to persuade and know the right time to pitch certain ideas to them and also find out the wrong times as well. When you can find out the right time to do certain things, you would be able to persuade people easily and without stress.

Time is something that not a lot of people take for granted. You may be looking for the right time to talk to a person, and when you finally do, you end up getting there late. You must take time very seriously, especially when you want to convince someone or a group of people.

Sometimes just you being there early shows the person you are trying to convince that you mean business, and you are not there to mess around with them. If you want to make them more impressed, you could be there a long time before they come in. When they get there and see you waiting even if they are early, they would feel bad and compelled to listen to you so that they do not waste much of your time. This is a technique that a lot of people take for granted.

The thing about time is that you do not know the events that would occur to make you late for an appointment, but you need to learn to anticipate the factors that may slow you down for an event or appointment. Some of these factors include:

- **Traffic**: This is one of the most common factors out there that can make you get to an appointment late, and the thing about traffic is that it could form at any day and anywhere, even in places where there is never traffic. If you really want to avoid traffic, especially in the mornings, look for places where there is little or no traffic and follow those routes at all times. But, if you must follow the roads that almost always have traffic, you can try and leave your house as early as you can before the traffic may begin to form.

If you can successfully get to your destination even before rush hour, you are gold. Sometimes your clients may even get stuck in traffic and start feeling bad that you may be waiting. There is no way he or she would not listen to you when they finally get there.

- **Neighbors**: Neighbors always have a way to slow you down, especially when you are going to work. It may be that they want to let you know something that happened during your absence or something that is going to happen when you are absent, and the funny thing is that some of them see that you are in a hurry to get out of the situation, but they want to talk to you by all means. If you want to get rid of neighbours like that all you have to do is be talking to them and at some point say, "I'm late for work, can we talk about this when I get back?" Anyone that hears this would know that you want to leave, and they may stop what they are saying for later or speed it up.

The main reason why people get held up by their neighbors is that they do not know how to tell them that they don't want to listen to them at that time. It is important that when you do this, it should be done as cleanly and nicely possible, meaning that you should not be rude when you are trying to leave the conversation, and you should not shut them up unnecessarily. If you want to let them know what it is you want to do, all you have to do is to say it politely, and before you know it, they would be out of your hair.

- **Kids**: A lot of parents would agree with this particular factor. When you have kids that go to school every day, you are bound to be late if you do not plan things very well. This could even be worse if the kids are still toddlers. Before you wake them up, bathe them, give them breakfast, and prepare them for school, there is a huge possibility that you are already late for your appointment. It is even worse when you are the one taking them to school.

If you want to avoid things like this, you need to get help. It could be a maid or maybe a family member that could come home that day to help you with the kids because of the appointment you would have to go to the next day. When you have someone to help you, you would be able to get things done easily and faster without stress at all. This does not mean that you should not do anything for them. It only means that you should not do everything for them. You could also get them to go with the school bus to avoid the risk of getting to your destination late.

There are still a lot of factors that could make you get to an appointment late, and you must find the loopholes in all these factors and use them to your advantage. When you can get out of the situation just by using the loopholes in them, there is a good chance that you would be able to get to any appointment without making your client wait for you for hours. Timing is one of the most important persuasion techniques and should not be taken for granted.

Exercise 6: Use Emotions To Your Advantage

This is something that not a lot of people know how to do. All some people do is talk and talk and talk without showing any emotions on their faces. When you want to convince someone, you should be able to make certain gestures with your face. You should not try to persuade someone to do something and say that the thing is going to make them happy, but meanwhile, you have the face of someone who got their dog killed. If you are trying to get someone to do something that you want, you do need to learn to back up your words with as little emotions and gestures as possible.

You do not need to keep a straight face from the beginning of the conversation until the end. Statistics show that some people are more interested in a conversation when they see some emotions in the face of the person trying to make those conversations happen. When you say something that requires a smile, smile. When you say something that requires you to be sad, then be sad. The thing is that if you don't know how to put proper emotions to your words, you are not going to be able to persuade someone effectively.

There are a lot of ways you can get your emotions to work in your favor. Some of those ways include:

- **Practice**: There are a lot of people out there that find it hard to put emotions in everything that they do. It may be because they do not know how to do it or because they never saw the need for it in the first place. Like everything that you are not used to, it would take some time to get used to, and that can only be done with a lot of practice.

  You can get to where you want to get to only if you practice enough, and this is no exception. If you want to learn how to talk with so much emotion, all you need is practice and a healthy dose of it for that matter. You could practice with friends and family members and ask them to grade you when you are done. Make sure that they give you honest answers and pointers so that you know where to brush up on your act. Your fake audience must be as real to you as possible, meaning that even if they are fake, you should think by all means that they are as real as they possibly can because if you think that they are not real, you are not going to take the practice seriously at all.

When you think that they are real, there is a huge chance that you are going to get better at using your emotions. You do not necessarily need to use a live audience to practice; the main reason why people use them is for feedback. You could also use your imagination to help you get what you want. You could imagine that the people that you want to speak to are standing right in front of you, and you need to speak to those imaginary people like they are real. Imagine their expressions and their looks and possibly everything they think that people would do in events like that. You must do this in front of a mirror or camera so that you can see how you look when you try to portray certain emotions as you talk.

It is important to know that this kind of practice does not work the first time you try it. Anyone that tells you otherwise is lying. You should know that if you want to get all of this right, you need to make sure that you spend weeks and maybe months to perfect it. This may seem like a lot, and sometimes you may think, "What is the need?" In the end, if you play your cards right, you would even be able to portray happy emotions when speaking to a client even when you are sad. You should know that time does not matter. All that matters is that you get what you want.

- **Help**: This may seem like a practice, but it is entirely different. Getting help in this context means getting professional help. Some people do not even know how to smile even when they are happy, and you should know that problems like that cannot be solved by talking to a friend or a family member.

The practice may not even work if you do not tackle the initial cause of your problem in the first place. The thing you need at this point is some professional help, and therapy is something you should try so that you would be able to know the main reason why you are unable to show emotions while you speak. This may seem unimportant, but it is very important and can be a very serious problem if not tackled sooner or later.

When you know what is wrong with you, there is a huge chance that you would be able to tackle certain problems that may come under that particular problem. Your therapy session should be centered on the main reason why you cannot tap into your emotions while you speak. There are real stories of people that are unable to cry no matter the situation.

There was an interview that was conducted on a person like that, and she said that she found out from her therapy session that the reason why she was unable to cry was that her mother always held her mouth when she wanted to cry when she was little. There is no way she would have had the ability to tackle that problem if she hadn't known the cause of the problem in the first place. If you can get all of this to help you talk to people better, you are a step closer to understanding the real art of persuasion.

All of the exercises listed above are known to help a lot of people persuade other people to do things that they would never have done on their own in the first place. If you are going to be able to pull this off, you need to do it with a lot of practice because nothing good comes easy. Even if you already know how to persuade someone, you still need to practice using these exercises. That is, if you want to be completely perfect at what you do.

Chapter 4: Practical Exercises For Mind Control

Mind control is a phenomenon that has fascinated many scientists over the years. It gives a person the ability to plant certain ideas and thoughts in the mind of another and activate them with the help of a trigger or a set of triggers. It is important to know that not everyone can be mind-controlled. For some, it may be difficult, while for others, it may be virtually impossible, so you should know that these exercises would not work for everyone, but they would be able to help you get in the minds of some people and control them in certain ways. Some of these techniques and exercises include the following.

Exercise 1: Conversational Hypnosis

As the name implies, it is a way of communicating with a person's unconscious mind without the person knowing at all. The main reason why it is called conversational hypnosis is that it is mostly done during a conversation. This means that you could be in a place having a regular conversation with a person, not knowing that the person is trying to hypothesize you. If you are carrying out this kind of hypnosis, you need to make your conversation as clear and clean as possible.

Covert hypnosis, as it is most often called, is a very subtle way to take control of the mind of a person at all times. Just like every other mind-control technique out there, covert hypnosis is not going to work on just anyone, but if you want to start the procedure on a person or a group of people, there are some things that you need to ensure before doing anything at all.

Firstly, you need to make sure that the person you are trying to hypnotize has focused attention and always responds to your suggestions. There is no way that you are going to get into a person's mind using this technique if the person does not have a good focus on anything, especially when it comes to the things that you say. It is called conversational hypnosis for a reason.

The person you are trying to hypnotize needs to be focused on the conversation that you both are having. Otherwise, there is no chance of it working. Also, suggestions are very important. The person you are trying to hypnotize needs to be in line with every suggestion that you put in front of them, no matter how absurd it may be. If you try to hypnotize someone that always asks a lot of questions and does not want to hear or believe anything you have to say, there would be a big problem because that kind of person would not be able to be mind-controlled in any way at all. If you are trying to control the mind of another person using this technique, you must put things like this into consideration. They might mean the difference between getting what you want and failing miserably.

If your candidates meet these requirements, all you have to do is plant suggestions during your conversation and believe it or not, if there are completely into what you are saying, you would be able to make those suggestions their new thoughts successfully.

This kind of hypnosis is far from easy because you cannot do it on just anyone. You need to be able to find the right candidate. Someone that you know would be able to do the things that you want and not the things that they want, and if by any chance you can find someone like that, you would be able to plant certain ideas in their heads without them knowing. These ideas they would believe more than the things that they are seeing or can see with their own eyes. It is so true.

There are stories of people that were hypnotized and were meant to believe certain things, and when they came out of hypnosis, they believed things that had no evidence. Just imagine yourself going into hypnosis, and by the time you come out of it, you believe that at a time, there used to be whales that flew. You may believe something like this deeply — even more than the fact that we breathe in oxygen.

This thing here is how powerful conversational hypnosis can be. It may happen to you just like that without your knowledge at all. You may be sitting there having a good and calm conversation, not knowing that you are slowly but surely being hypnotized. If you are going to try this technique at all, you must know that you should never do it to plant bad ideas or suggestions in the minds of people.

If you must do this, do it as a way to plant good suggestions into the minds of people because you do not want to be Hitler at this point. Yes, there are stories of people that Hitler used mind control to get to. These people would go to places, do this, and also give information that they would not normally give if they were in their right minds.

When trying to perform this form of mind control, there are certain things that you should avoid. Some of them are:

- **Never try to hypnotize a person in a noisy place**: The key to hypnosis is the focus, and you should know that you are not going to be getting a lot of focus from the person you are trying to hypnotize when the place is so loud you can barely hear yourself. You need to be in a place that is as calm as possible. This does not mean that you must be in a place where nobody talks; it only means that you must be in a place where you both can hear each other talk. When you find a place like that, hypnosis is said to be easier.

- **Do not force your suggestions**: This is probably the last thing you want to do when you are trying to hypnotize a person. When you attempt to force your suggestions on a person, especially when the person is resisting, it breaks the focus of the person and when that is done, establishing that kind of focus again is virtually impossible, and if it does happen, it is going to take a longer period to establish.

Exercise 2: The Use of Hypnotic Keywords

Hypnosis is known as one of the most effective ways to control the minds of others, even if it cannot be used on just anyone. When you try to hypnotize a person to believe something that you want to believe, there are certain words that you could use to ensure that you are going to be getting what you want from them when the hypnotic state is over. Some of these words include the following:

- **Imagine**: This is a very powerful keyword in the art of hypnosis because it could make people believe the things that are not even there. It also makes people believe things that are far from real. How? Think about when you watch certain horror movies and in the movie, the ghost might take its victim when he or she is taking a shower.

  Suddenly you imagine that your shower looks like the one in the movie, and there is no way you are taking a shower anytime soon. You have imagined the possibility of that kind of thing happening to you. As such, you avoid situations where it might take place. The same thing goes for this kind of hypnosis. When you want to get into the mind of a person and control it, "imagine" is a word that you want to use because it is known as one of the most powerful hypnotic keywords amongst the rest.

When you use this keyword to your advantage during hypnosis, try not to use it a lot during one session so as not to throw yourself off your game. If you want to do it right, all you have to do is to know the right time to use it, and when you find that out, there is a huge chance that you are going to get those ideas in their minds with a lot of ease.

- **As**: This is a word that is used to make the person you are trying to hypnotize know what is happening to them then. No matter how far you have gone with a particular person, using this word would help you establish more when it comes to hypnosis. For instance, you could say, "As you are listening to my voice, you are beginning to understand, and as you begin to understand, your unconscious mind is now taking you into a deep trance".

You may think that there is virtually nothing that is going on as you are using this word, but you are so wrong because a lot is going on at a time. You are telling them what you want them to know, and because they do not know exactly what is going on, they tend to believe you and continue with everything that you are saying. This is why you see a lot of hypnotists use this word.

Hypnotic keywords are like every other word out there, meaning that there is nothing special to them. You do not have to think that because they are called power words, they do not have the same feeling as every other word. You would be wrong. These words are just like our everyday day words out there.

There is nothing special to any of them at all. They all have the same meaning, and they all serve the same purpose, but the key to the words is how they are used. This is what a lot of people do not understand. When you are trying to hypnotize a person with these words, you can succeed or fail depending on how you use the words.

If you use the words the right way they are supposed to be used, you are going to get more than you ever imagined because you may be able to get people to fall into a trance faster than you have ever imagined. But, if you do not use the words properly, you would not be making any impact on the person that you are trying to hypnotize.

The thing about keywords that makes them so important is that they tend to create a link between the subconscious and conscious mind which means that it would be easier to get into the minds of people with the words that link their two minds together. This is one of the reasons why people take years and years trying to practice and perfect getting the right words to talk to the right people.

If you want to understand this concept better and use it to your advantage, you must practice with a lot more words as often as possible because the more you practice, the easier it would be for you to get into the minds of people and control them at will.

If you are going to be using these words, you should know that all these words do not work for everyone; this is why you must use the words very carefully. When you are using a particular word on a person, and you notice that the word you are using is making little or no impact on the person, you can always change it up a bit with other words. How do you know when the words are not working? You would know when the person you are trying to hypnotize is not buying any of your suggestions.

When some people think about mind control, the only thing that practically jumps into their minds is controlling the mind of another person. You should know that mind control can work both ways. You can control your mind and make yourself do things that you would not normally do. Some people would never see themselves doing something like exercising, and if you are that kind of person, you should know that the reason why you don't see yourself doing that is because of the way your mind is. You have unconsciously restructured your mind around the fact that you would never exercise, no matter how many times you are being asked to.

If you want to see yourself exercise, all you have to do is sit down and control your mind. Tell your mind what you want it to do, and it would do it. After all, it is called your mind for a reason. There are different ways that you can successfully control your mind. Some of these ways include:

Exercise 3: Avoid Worrying Thoughts

There are a lot of reasons why a person would want to spend all day thinking about something that happened before or is going to happen. It may be because of their spouse, money, and so much more. If you are the kind of person that spends all day or night thinking about something that has practically no meaning, you should know that it is all because of the structure of your mind.

The mind is a place where even the impossible can become possible, no matter how irrational it may look in reality. There are some tricks that you can use to make yourself stop any form of harmful rumination, and they include:

- **Create a "worry" time**: When you tend to create time for your problems, there is a huge chance that you would solve them during that time, which means that you would not need to worry about them even when you do not want to. You can do this at any time of the day, but it needs to be at a time where you would not have anyone around you to create any form of distractions.
- **Take a walk**: Taking a walk may seem basic, but it can also be seen as one of the most effective ways to get your mind off a lot of stressful things. When you go out and take a walk, you see different things, hear different sounds, and so much more. The thing is that your mind is going to be a lot less occupied with your worries when it

is trying to view a whole lot of other things. You could do this with a pet or a family member. The objective here is to do this with a person that relaxes you as well.

- **Think of the worst thing that could happen**: This may sound like you jumping into something that you do not want to jump into but when you do this, all you need to do is to imagine yourself solving that particular problem in the worst-case scenario, and if you are able to do that, you will notice that may have solved the real problem and probably found out the main reason why you have been having that problem in the first place.

Exercise 4: Believe In Yourself At All Times

Believing in yourself could be one of the best and easiest ways to control your mind. Some people always believe that they are not good enough, and they are not going to amount to anything in life. You may think that these people want to think this way, but they do not. There is a possibility that a series of events in their lives have made them believe less of themselves. But they can easily get out of that situation.

All that they feel and tell themselves is as a result of what the mind tells them at all times. You can control your mind into believing what you want it to believe, and that can easily be done by believing in yourself. All you have to do is to sit down and tell yourself things that uplift your spirit and soul.

You may think that this is not going to have any effect. But if you can stand in front of a mirror and tell yourself that you are good at what you do over and over again, your mind would be forced to believe it. And just like that, you have succeeded in controlling your mind.

Exercise 5: Never Blame Yourself

This may not look like a way to control the mind, but it is. The mind can make you blame yourself for things that you know that you have little or no control over.

You may be sitting at home, and you get a call from your child's school that your child fell and got injured. Instead of asking if he or she is ok, you begin to blame yourself for everything when you know there is no way you could take care of your child from home—unless you want to fit your child with a camera. If something happens and it was not your fault or beyond your control, just let it go. When you learn to avoid personalization, you now gain certain power over your mind, which means that you would now be able to control your mind with no stress at all.

Controlling your mind is not something that is easy and should not be seen as that. You cannot control your mind if you are not able to put aside some certain things and get your head in the game. This is probably the reason why a lot of people find it hard in the first place. The thing here is that if you are not able to put important things in front of the unimportant ones, there is absolutely no way you are going to be able to control your mind without stress. Even if you succeed in controlling your mind, you would always go back if you do not make the necessary adjustments.

Just like every other phenomenon out there, if you want to get something like this right, you need to practice as much as you can. The more you practice, the better you get at it. Should it all go the exact way you had planned it, you could become so proficient at mind control that you're able to teach others to control their minds. What a plus!

Chapter 5: Practical Exercises That Can Be Used To Prevent Mind Control

The real question here is why, in the first place, would anyone want to control your mind? Some people may not want to check out some of these exercises because they feel like there would be no reason for a person to try to control their minds in the first place, but you must know that there are a lot of reasons why people may want to control your mind. Some of the reasons why people would want to control your mind include:

- **They want you to get something for them**: It may be money, documents, or any other thing. The reason why they have chosen you is that they know you are the only one that can get it for them. As such, you become their mind control project. There are even stories of people that say that they were robbed one way or the other, but when they checked the security tapes, the people who called the police were the robbers. Sounds strange, right? A professional can get you to rob your own house and plant a bomb in there by yourself, even if you have no bomb training.

- **They may want information**: This is another reason why someone would want to hypnotize you. You do not necessarily need to have money for someone to need something from you. They may need access codes or maybe the names of people in a place. What they want to do with the information is a total mystery, but the thing is that you might have succeeded in telling them things that you would not normally tell them if you were not hypnotized in the first place.

Mind control is something that a lot of people would love to learn, but not a lot of people want their minds to be controlled by another person in any way. If you are that kind of person, there are certain things that you need to learn to do so that you would not fall victim to any form of mind control. Some of these things are bound to work at all times, while some of them would only work for just a handful of people. No two people are exactly the same, as you already know by now. And different people require different techniques. Some of these practical exercises include:

Exercise 1: Do Not Keep Your Eyes In One Position

People who tend to control the minds of others can be very skilled at times. Some of them would want to use everything they can to get your attention to persuade you and control your mind at all times. When you notice that you are in the presence of someone that wants to control your mind, try as much as possible to keep your eyes in random motion. Do not let your eyes focus on one thing at the same time, especially if that thing is something that they are holding.

There are various ways a person can control your mind, and your eyes are a good gateway for that to happen. You do not want your gateway to be wide open and for you to be defenseless when someone is trying to get into your mind. When someone is trying to control your mind, and you notice, all you have to do is avoid any kind of eye contact with them.

Do not let them think that they can get to you with your eyes because when they do, they will use that technique against you almost every single time. When people like that find your weak point, they tend to exploit it no matter how many times you try to hide it. This is why you mustn't let them know what that is in the first place.

There are certain things that you should not do when you are trying to avoid eye contact with the person trying to control your mind. These things are said to be very important and should not be taken for granted. Some of these things include:

- **Don't let them know**: You should never let the person that is trying to control your mind know that you know what he or she is doing and most importantly, do not let them know that you are aware of their technique because when they know that you are aware of their technique, they will tend to change it immediately and they might still be able to get you one way or the other. If you want to be able to get out of that problem, all you have to do is act oblivious.

- **Don't get distracted**: Getting distracted around a person who is trying to control your mind is the last thing you want to do when it comes to avoiding them. When you want to avoid something like mind control, you need to make sure that you are alert at all times. When you are avoiding the eyes of the people who are trying to control you, you mustn't forget and mistakenly gaze at them again because that might be your downfall. Keep your mind and body alert at all times because the moment you let your guard down, they would not hesitate to take advantage of you.

If you can keep your eyes in constant random motion and at the same time avoid all these pointers, there is a good chance that no one would be able to get into your mind no matter how many times they try. You should know that some professionals would go out of their way to get to you, but if you stick to all that you need to do, you would be one of their biggest challenges. If you play your cards right, you may be able to confuse them to the point that they would have to leave you alone and go for much easier targets. How do you confuse them? When they are trying to get to you with your eyes, let them get to the point that they think that they have almost gotten you and make them know that they are still a long way from penetrating your mind. Once they notice that the closer they are to getting to your mind, the harder it gets, they would get confused because you would become a harder nut to crack.

You must know that this takes a lot of practice as well. You cannot just wake up one morning and say that you are not going to be able to be mind-controlled, but if you practice enough and take the right precautions at the right time, there is a good chance that you are not going to be able to be controlled by anyone, but if you are going to be controlled in any way, it is not going to be easy for the people trying to control you and your mind.

This is only but one exercise that can be used to prevent mind control. Others may be equally effective or more effective as the case may be.

Exercise 2: Don't Let People Copy Your Body Language

This is probably something that you thought was far from important, but it is. If you are in the presence of a person trying to control your mind and you find out the person is sitting in the way you are seated, or the person is mirroring your movements in any way, keep it in mind that the person is trying to get inside your mind in some way. This is why it is important to mind your surroundings at all times because they could get to you just by mirroring your hand gestures.

You may not notice them doing this because they can be subtle as they possibly can. If you even come in contact with the professionals, there is a huge chance that you are not going to be able to find out what they are up to until it is too late to go back. It is important to know that you may be able to figure the person out if that person is new in the game.

The thing is that professionals are very clean in their game, so clean that you may not know what they are doing until they are done, but when it comes to a rookie, you can be able to spot what he or she is doing almost immediately because they are not as clean as the professionals. A professional would mirror your movements and gestures very quietly, meaning that you would never catch them doing it, but a rookie on the other hand may tend to change his or her gestures immediately. You change yours. That's right, there is a huge giveaway. When you notice something like that happening around you, know that the person you are dealing with is a big-time rookie, and all you have to do is to mess with them and have fun with it. You can change your gestures and movements as often as possible and watch them get confused and break down.

As usual, there are certain things that you do not want to be doing when a person is trying to mirror your movements in any way at all. These things include:

- **Never sit in one place**: This is probably the last thing you want to do, especially if the person trying to mirror you is right in front of you. When you are in the presence of someone like that, all you have to do is keep moving around. You do not need to move around like a mad person. If not, they would know that you have made them.

Just move around casually like you have no idea what is going on around you, and if you can be in as many places as possible and still make as many gestures as possible, there is a good chance that they are not going to be able to see where you are going. Some of them may get so frustrated and decide to get your attention by subtly standing in front of you so that you forget what exactly you are doing, but when they do, you can always change your gestures over and over again to mess with their heads.

- **Mind your surroundings**: This may be hard for some people because there are a lot of people out there that find it so hard to mind their surroundings no matter how long you try to teach them. This is because they are more focused on the things happening right in front of them and fail to see the things happening around them.

If you are that kind of person, getting into your mind would be a piece of cake because if you want to notice someone trying to get you, you have to be aware of your surroundings with every chance you get. Do not see something strange on the road or in your house and just let it go like that. Try as much as possible to investigate even if you do not get there by yourself.

The bottom line to all of this is that if you know what is going on around you, you would be able to tackle and address it before it becomes too late, and when you address it early enough, there is absolutely no way that a person can easily control your mind.

It is imperative to know that these tips would not work for everyone, and you must also know that you would not be able to get the best results out of this if you practice it repeatedly. The reason why you need to practice in this context is that there are a lot of skilled mind control specialists out there, and you need to be on your game at all times. You do not need to sit down thinking that no one can get into your mind just because you have succeeded in successfully spotting one or two of them coming your way. There is a good chance that you are going to meet a person that is more than a professional. These kinds of mind control specialists that do not need to get close to you to know what you are doing and control your mind.

Some of these kinds of people can come to you, and the only thing they have to do is to say a word to you, and that word may be able to trigger some series of events, and before you know it, you are under the control of someone you just met.

Exercise 3: Always Be Aware Of Strange Language

This is another technique that people who are trying to control your mind use. This does not necessarily mean that they are going to use another language like French, for example. These people are going to say some things to you. Things that you do not know the meaning of, things that you do not hear every day. It may be a word or group of words, but the thing is that they believe that if you do not know what they are saying, it would be easier for them to put different ideas into your head and at the same time, try to hypnotize you.

These people tend to use vague language on you, and without you noticing at all, you may be slowly slipping into a trance. This process is known to take as little time as possible, which means that the person does not have to talk to you for a very long time before they put you in a trance. It could happen with just the snap of a finger.

You must know that this kind of mind control cannot only be done in person. The key here is the voice of the person that is trying to control your mind. All they have to do is talk to you, whether on the phone or not. The only thing they want you to do is to hear their voice and listen to all the vague things that they want you to say, and if you do not know or you know and decide to forget about it, you would be falling into their trap.

The reason why this technique works very well is because people that know how to control minds also know how to talk and all they have to do is to find that sweet spot where you literally do not know what is going on anymore, and when they have that they would not hesitate to exploit it for their gain. You can see all of this coming from a mile away, and you can avoid it if you see it on time, but it won't be easy. There are some techniques that you could use to get out of their trap, and they include:

- **Never pretend you understand**: This is where a lot of people get it wrong and end up getting hypnotized one way or the other. The thing is that if you do not know what a person is saying and you feel like the person is saying it to plant ideas in your head, leave the conversation as fast as you can.

  It would take only a few minutes for someone very skilled in mind control to get into your head without any stress at all. If you are talking with a person or a group of people and you notice that they start using some vague language on you, do not pretend you know it at all.

  This is because the more you pretend, the easier it is for them to figure out your mind. So when you are in a conversation and you do not understand, all you have to do is to try and let the person speaking with you know that you do not understand and if they don't stop, just end the conversation because if you stay there nodding your head over and over again for words you do not understand you may end up doing things that you don't remember why you're doing. Because you were hypnotized.

This particular technique is probably the only thing you can do to make sure that you do not fall in the hands of people who are trying to control your mind in any way. When you begin to understand that even the slightest word or group of words can easily get you hypnotized, there is no way you are going to be able to let your guard down at all. If you want to make more out of this, practice ending conversation with other people and be amazed at the results.

Chapter 6: Understanding Manipulation

Almost every one of us must have been in this position. A person comes to you to either make a request that seemed reasonable or advise you to make a decision that in their words is "for your own good". Meanwhile, you are not comfortable with it and your insides are burning up. That feeling is common when we are experiencing a manipulation attempt by someone.

However, these things cannot actually be prevented, as people use a lot of manipulation tactics too often. Manipulation is the exertion of inappropriate influence on a person, trying to exploit them emotionally and mentally so as to gain power, control, or enjoy certain benefits or privileges at their expense.

Manipulating is not the same thing as "social influence" because the latter does not need anyone to force it. A social influencer does not need to cause harm to a person before influencing their choices or preferences. However, manipulators would want to cause power imbalance so they will have the power to take advantage of people's weaknesses and pursue their own personal desires.

Manipulation can be done by anybody including those who are very close to us like family members, friends, lovers, and even our children. Since manipulation tactics are even closer to us than we think, how then can we identify who is manipulating us and when they are doing it? It is usually tough being around a person who is manipulative because they can be draining, and induce a lack of self-confidence in you.

It is not so easy to detect when someone is manipulating us, but then we can at least try to analyze their behavior and know if people are doing things for manipulative purposes or not. These are some of the characteristics used to identify a manipulative individual.

1. They Find It Easy To Guilt Trip: A manipulative person does not understand the concept of accepting blame. Instead, they'll try to push over the blame to you or guilt-trip you. It is very possible that you did nothing wrong to them, but they will try to shift the feelings to you and make you feel guilty and terrible about the situation.

They easily turn things on you and make you feel like you don't care even when you do. Manipulators can make you feel as though you don't care and they can even make you feel terrible and guilty for being in a better position or having more in life than they do, all these things being something you have little or no control over. Their attitude may make you develop anxiety and guilt and sometimes, you could also develop self-doubt.

2. Manipulative People Will Gradually Erode Your Self Confidence: Usually, manipulators will desire that you have only small or no self-confidence because this will make them have more power over you. They will be able to break you until you feel less than them.

A manipulative person will comment about things that affect your self-confidence, knowing fully well that it will increase your self-consciousness and may destroy you. This could be done by people very close to you. When they are able to bring you to a low point, they'll feel better about themselves and will then find it easy to take advantage of you.

This will make you feel even sadder and negative and the only way you can save your situation is by learning about how to rid your life of negative people.

3. They Do Not Acknowledge Blame: A lot of manipulative people will refuse to accept blame for things they did. Instead, they'll want to shift the blame to you, even when you had no hand in the situation. They will do what they can to make you feel that you've committed an offense so grievous. This gives them even more power to exploit you.

This will always be a heavy weight for you to carry, especially if you are in a relationship or friend group, because your manipulator will never take the blame for anything while you keep taking the blame even when it is not your fault. This can stress you out, make you anxious, and you won't know how to get released from this emotional torture because the manipulative person will always try to maintain that power that they have.

4. Manipulative People Will Often Easily Switch Subjects: Manipulative people often always care about only themselves. This means that whenever you are having an argument or discussion that threatens to expose their manipulative traits, they'll easily change the subject or switch topics.

If they notice they are the wrongdoers, they will turn the conversation away and soon it will rest on you or something that does not relate to the conversation at all. That way they can avoid the truth, avoid receiving blame, and still have the power to control you in the situation.

This might plunge you into a state of hopelessness knowing that there's no way you can win, so you resign and keep up with the other conversation and still give them the power to take advantage of you. This actually shows that what you intend to say has nothing to do with them and they are emotionally unavailable except it is going to benefit them.

5. Manipulators Rationalise Their Behaviour: Whenever a manipulative person does wrong, they will still not show it. They will still find a way to make them look good and rationalize that act they portrayed. When they do this, they will always be right despite any argument you throw at them because they are prepared to rationalize their behavior.

Because of this, they will not pay heed to anything you have to say to them but will allow you finish making your points, then they will justify themselves for their actions and make you agree that their behavior was right. A manipulator is always right and their behavior is always fine and justified even though it isn't.

How To Use Manipulation Techniques

There are times when you need something so badly that you have to manipulate people into getting it. This means that you have to be able to analyze people and know which technique to use best. However, these are some of the top techniques that you can use to navigate your life in your best interest.

1. The Fear-And-Relief Technique: Basically, this fear and relief technique has a lot to do with toying with the emotions of the other person. Although this technique can lead to a lot of stress and anxiety, it works very well.

There are just two simple steps to follow:

The first thing to do is to create something that the other person will fear. This makes them very vulnerable and you can spin that vulnerability to your benefit. Try to offer them something to relieve that fear that they are experiencing.

This tactic is only difficult because you have to know what to scare the individual with. There is no way that you'll be able to scare them by bringing up scary things on the spot thinking that they will develop fear on the spot. You have to have an idea of what you'll say and how you'll say it beforehand. Then you will also need to create that solution that will rescue them from the uncomfortable feeling that you'll create.

This tactic is one of the ways that the media tries to keep viewers hitched to their station. For instance, the news channel can put up a piece of scary news about a very dramatic announcement. They could talk about a new virus outbreak plaguing the city which will definitely instill fear into people. They usually end the news with advice to the viewers to remain glued to the station if they want more information on how to evade the deadly virus. Now they have swiftly created a solution to the fear they caused.

Since you are not a news channel, you may think this technique is irrelevant to you, but you can use it to make people scared of things. It could be their relationships or career goals. Just think of something creative, study your target, and present a better way of doing the method for yourself.

At the point when the person is showing signs of giving up, then you try to come to their aid as they seek ways to relieve the stress and blow off steam. What you do then is to disarm the person by plunging them into mood swings. This will make them even more open to doing whatever it is you require from them and they will eventually do it.

2. Mirroring technique: A lot of people often use this technique. It has two parts. At first, you are the one mirroring that person who you intend to influence and after that, they will be the one to mirror you.

This helps to build a bond and trust between you and that person and it creates a rapport that you will ultimately have to exploit. This is basic and easy to do. First, you copy the behavior of the person. Notice their body language, hand gestures, facial expressions and the tone of voice used. Are they standing with their hands crossed? Stand the same way. Are they making quiet conversations without showing many emotions? Talk in the same manner.

However, while you're all about copying their actions, do it with as much care as you can. If you make it so obvious that you have been observing and mirroring this person, they will become suspicious of you. This will be a bad thing for you because you won't make any progress with them.

Now, assuming you are able to mirror them undetected, the person will begin to feel that they are connected to you. It is at this time that they'll trust you strongly, creating a chance and making themselves vulnerable to the manipulation. One very amazing thing you'll notice is that they will now begin to mirror your own behavior. If this happens, then you have been able to complete the trust-building process.

If you want to push your manipulation farther, then you should master this technique because you can easily influence a person. As long as a rapport has been created, you can successfully start using the other methods available. Ensure that your mirroring takes time and does not hope to succeed with everything after just a few minutes of trying. Sometimes you can keep trying for hours before the person warms up to you

3. Use the guilty approach: This is one proven way to effectively manipulate a person. The power of making someone feel guilty about something, whether it's their fault or not, should not be undermined. A person who feels guilty about anything will try their best to make compensations for it. If you put them in that position, then it will be much easier for you to suggest your own ideas to them.

At this point, you're subtly filling their subconscious mind with your own ideas and waiting until they are able to flow with the tide. You can successfully use this tactic on those people who can easily feel guilty either because they have betrayed your trust once or they have disappointed you in the past.

But then, using guilt to manipulate people is not so hidden. It is quite obvious that you are doing what you do because you want something and if care is not taken, the people around you may suspect that you are being manipulative. But despite that, it works very well and is an easy technique.

This is more about reminding the person to do something for you by referring to things you have done for them in the past or making them feel bad for disappointing you and refusing to do something to compensate you.

4. Play the victim card: Playing the victim is something you can do together with the guilt technique. If you want maximum satisfaction and results, then try to combine both methods. What you should be careful about, though, is the fact that playing the victim card can also turn out to be unfavorable for you if you do it. Be careful not to overuse it.

This is a simple scenario where you present yourself as their victim and try to make them feel as though they are instructing you. You can do this by making them feel like they are the ones doing the manipulation.

You can talk about how you do not deserve to get the treatment they are giving you. You may even ask them if they treat everybody bad or they are just being that way to you because they hate you. You can even try to appeal to their conscience by asking them what wrong you committed to make them treat you this way.

These kinds of words make people feel that they are resisting you and being rude. Because of the guilt they feel, they will become nicer to you and eventually turn out to do your wishes.

5. Love bombing method: This kind of emotional manipulation tactic is used mostly by narcissists. They use it during the early stages of interaction with the person that will be influenced. All you do is show a lot of positive affection and attention to them and they'll be drawn to you because they see you as a good person.

Naturally, humans will treat people who show them love nicely and soon they will fall deep into the emotional space you have created for them. The victim begins to open up and create some feelings for you and they are clouded by the positive stance you take.

However, don't expect the love-bombing method to work for everybody around. Don't just try to use one method for everyone. The people who are most vulnerable to the love-bombing method are those who already desire love and affection from people. When a person is already lonely and seeks to interact with other people positively, then they are easily vulnerable to this technique.

However, after using the method and seeing it work, you should take it easy with the next steps you'd take. Don't make your intentions clear early enough and don't flash a fake smile around for a few minutes and then proceed to request what you want. You'll be easily detected.

A lot of groups and cults use the love-bombing methods on their members and they easily attract millions to themselves. First, they are so nice to you and you may or may not think about the intentions they have because they are skilled at hiding so they don't scare people away.

However, after a certain time when you have been successfully cajoled into registering with their group, they'll show their manipulative fangs but because you have been carried away with their positive approach and you no longer understand what's happening, you will be easily swayed.

6. Try the bribery technique: This manipulation method is also one that works quite well. Whenever you reward a person, it will make them feel obligated to do the same for you. You can use this in your own interest.

What you need to do is find out the things that your friend or acquaintance wants and just provide it for them. After that, make a suggestion about wanting to get something back. However, make sure that you don't make it look as though you're blackmailing them. They'll see through you and you won't like the outcome. Make sure you present yourself as a person who wants to be really nice to them.

This technique is very easy to use as long as you don't make it clear what your real intentions are. All you do is pretend that you're a nice person just so that when you give out the stuff you want to, people will see it as a nice gesture. This manipulation technique is used by people ranging from salespeople, to marketing departments, and others who seek favor. From studies done by experts, when people get a small favor from others they are moved to do an even bigger favor.

You can only get this done by timing. You should know the time when people want things and what they want so that the things you're giving out to them will be important.

You can't just give your boss something like a pen in exchange for a promotion just in one hour. You have to be careful because you need to have the trust and connection of the people you want to influence before you influence them.

Also, don't think you have to buy people expensive things before you can win them over. It can be with little things like getting them free coffee once in a while or sharing your sweets with them occasionally. This will make them have a relaxed attitude with you and when you request something, they'll have the mentality that you're a nice person to them and they'll want to help you.

7. Become a good listener and actually learn a lot about a person: Manipulators are not magicians who just whisper a few magic words or use some code words to take over your brain and control you the way they want. That's not how it works.

If you want to use their tactics, then you'll need to develop trust and connection between you and the person of interest. When someone does not trust, they will not want to collaborate with you on anything, and that means it is no longer possible for you to influence them. This is the reason why you should be their friend. How better to do that than be a good listener? There are two ways being a good listener helps you influence people:

- When you're a good listener, the person perceives some amount of friendship during the conversation. When people notice that you are interested in the things they say, you become more trustworthy and appealing. People who do not have a lot of social interactions will easily welcome you into their lives because of their desperation for companionship. They'll tell you about their lives, talk about the things they did some hours back, where their next vacation spot will likely be, and go as far as opening up their intimate life to you. You don't even have to do much but listen quietly. If you don't like what you hear and it's boring, just make them think that you are interested.

- They begin to develop much trust towards you when at some point during the conversation, you're able to recall and tell them something that they have once told you. When you do this, they'll begin to believe that you were actually showing genuine care and you were listening.

If the conversation was boring, there's a chance that you won't find it easy to remember the things they said during the conversation because you actually wanted to manipulate them. But try as much as you can not to forget some necessary details. If they were saying a lot about their vacation, you don't have to tell them everything about it, you can just casually note how the vacation went.

8. Learn to read people's body language: Body language is very important and necessary for influencing people. People give out a lot of expressions about how they feel through the body language that they use instead of words.

Whenever you think you are taking too much time to understand what a person does, just focus your attention on their body language. People consider reading body language to be art. For you to totally have the power to manipulate a person effortlessly, you should be able to find out how that person is made up emotionally and psychologically. You would need to learn a lot of features about them including their body language. It is easy or convenient for people to lie and twist what they say very easily, but then they cannot hide or lie about the signs that their body is sending.

Another thing you should consider is that people easily respond to emotions more than other things. When the person you're targeting to influence is a very emotional one, then you do not have any choice but to play with their emotions.

Reading body language is not a complicated activity but then it is necessary and one of the basic things that you'll need if you want to manipulate another person.

It does not have any secret code or any hidden thing you must do before you master how to use people's body expressions in influencing people. Some of the basic expressions that you should look out for include:

When you see someone who has crossed their arms, whose face seems devoid of expression and avoids eye contact with other people, then it shows his disinterest in having any conversation with anybody. It can also mean that the person is going through stress, is angry, or unhappy.

If a person is relaxed and near you with an emotional facial expression and keeps making prolonged eye contact, then it means they want to be engaged, are in a positive mood, and will be open to having a conversation with you.

9. Use your looks in your best interest: It doesn't matter how we judge people, but human nature has a degree of shallowness. Humans are naturally wired to be attracted to people with charisma. When you have good looks, it is quite easy for you to put it to good use and influence other people. Truly, life is not so hard for those with good looks, but then you don't have to rely only on that to go far. You need to put in extra effort and learn how to make it help you grow.

Together with your charisma, you also have to develop a positive and cheerful attitude, and also have body language that does not put people off. When you successfully make this happen, then you can reap the benefits in your personal dealings and professional life. Make people feel as though they have something special in them and always portray yourself as having self-confidence. However, you don't have to do it excessively because, despite your charisma, people will not want to associate with you if you are cocky.

10. You should target their feelings but ensure that you have mastered your own first: If you want to manipulate people easily, make them fall in love with you. Monitor them closely and anytime that person stops being rational and starts being emotional, then you should be ready to make your move and have them do what it is you want from them. Before you do that, you need to first act as their guide and endure that they have developed certain feelings towards you. A lot of people who have perfected the art of manipulation like to use this tactic because if you are not able to control your own emotions, you might be the one who ends up being manipulated. You should know how to create both sympathy and fear without having to fall into the trap you made for others. That, however, is the difficult part, but you can learn it.

Conclusion

How was all that? I truly hope the information in this book and the way it was delivered proved to be useful to you. Many days of hard work went into writing this book. The information had to be tested and relevant. But that's my bit done. If this book will bring any positive change to your life, you must also work. Don't just read the exercises and stop at applauding or criticizing. Actually try them out for yourself.

You don't have to settle for limitations, and this is the moral of this book. Very few things can stand in the way of someone who can protect their minds from manipulation and effectively persuade anyone.

References

Bloom, S. (2018). Activities for nonverbal communication. Retrieved from

> https://bizfluent.com/4934834/activities-for-nonverbal-communication

Forsey, C. (n.d.). How to handle manipulative coworkers, managers and clients like a

> pro. Retrieved from https://blog.hubspot.com/marketing/manipulators

Hill, R. (n.d.). How to manipulate people - expert manipulation techniques. Retrieved

> from https://www.psychologium.com/7-ways-to-manipulate-someone-to-do-anything-you-want/amp/

Maharjan, P. (2018). Activities related to nonverbal communication. Retrieved from

> https://www.businesstopia.net/communication/non-verbal-communication-activities

Price, L. (2016). Nonverbal communication exercises for the drama class. Retrieved

> from https://www.theatrefolk.com/blog/nonverbal-communication-exercises/

Segal, J., Smith, M., et al. (2019). Nonverbal communication. Retrieved from

> https://www.helpguide.org/articles/relationships-communication/nonverbal-communication.htm